PHILADELPHIA

A HIKER'S PARADISE

by

VICTOR GROVE

Published by
Northern Liberties Press
Old City Publishing Inc.
628 North 2nd Street
Philadelphia, PA 19123, USA

Visit our web site at: oldcitypublishing.com

ISBN 1-933153-01-6

Printed in the United States.

PHILADELPHIA
A HIKER'S
PARADISE

BY

VICTOR GROVE

northern liberties press
**Philadelphia, Paris
Kuala Lumpur, London**

PARK
ENTRANCE

INTRODUCTION

My husband put this little volume together to celebrate the Bicentennial. However, 30 years ago the time was not yet ripe. Only for a few this treasure had become a haven, a retreat, a replacement for ill-affordable vacations. For most others the Wissahickon Valley was a totally blank page.

While living downtown, almost every weekend we could be found hiking in the thicket, finding new trails, and of course a special place-with-a-view for our picnic lunch. Only a few were aware of this remarkable treasure, begging to be used. Our hearts would beat with joy, when occasionally, someone, smilingly greeting, would pass by.

You would not wonder, then, that this is where it had to be: RIGHT BY THE PARK, when we began looking for a home of our own. Of course, there we created our own large garden. But our hikes in the Wissahickon had become a part of our life. Nothing could replace that.

So it might not be more than a step up, that after several years into widowhood, selling the home, and encountering great difficulties finding a suitable place to live, against all odds I should finally be presented with keys to an apartment right by the park. I believe it was once a part of it, the abundance of trees bearing witness to that, with its sign of **PARK ENTRANCE** right on the grounds. But the crowning glory of it all? My new apartment number is no other than my husband's date of birth.

To live in a busy, crowded polluted city, yet feel as if you were by the Harz Hills and beautiful Waterfalls in Europe; able to get there at a moment's notice after a day's work, or even before, at the price of a bus-fare, is indeed a unique situation we here in Philadelphia are priviledged with. For too long a time we have ignored what we already possess, treated it as if it were nothing. While actually it is Philadelphia's PRICELESS TREASURE.

Herta Grove

FOREWORD

This collection is meant to pay homage to a unique feature of the American scene: the Wissahickon Valley. Indeed, together with Fairmount Park it forms the largest green belt within any city in the world.

About its stream, the Wissahickon, Edgar Allan Poe said "that it was so remarkable a loveliness, that were it flowing in England, it would be the theme of every bard and the common topic of every tongue."

Surprising as it may seem, there are still far too many people in this city who are not aware of its jewel. The manager of a local drugstore, for instance, where some of the photos reproduced here were developed, was so impressed that he exclaimed, "O, you have been to Europe!" He was hard to convince that the photos were taken in an area only a few minutes walk from his doorstep.

As this happens to be quite a frequent reaction, it is my hope that this little publication, the harvest of a great number of hikes, may help to remedy this somewhat regrettable state of affairs. It may persuade people that they do not have to board a jumbo jet and fly to the ends of the earth to find natural scenes like these, scenes which have remained practically unchanged since the days when the Lenape Indians were the only human beings who found peace and a sense of belonging in these woods. Can you think of any metropolis where you can walk for miles without meeting a soul, without seeing human habitations, being surrounded by thousands of trees, accompanied by a gently flowing creek?

It is understood, however, that a person who wants to enjoy this unexpected reserve of nature must follow Poe's advice and "walk. He must leap ravines, he must risk his neck among precipices." Of course, there are many good trails which do not entail any risk to life or limb, and there are even comfortable paths where no cars will disturb your stroll or pollute the air. In fact, every hiker will get his share of "the truest, the richest, and most unspeakable glories of the land."

Even a short exploration of this "valley in the city" must leave any visitor with the conviction that it is worth coming to Philadelphia for this experience alone - to say nothing of all the other attractions this city has to offer - and the tired old joke, first prize one week and second prize two weeks in Philadelphia, will appear in all its ludicrousness.

The quotations selected for these pictures reflect the heritage of this country. They may even encourage you to go for a walk in the woods with Emerson, or Thoreau, or William Penn - and a camera. The universal insights expressed in some of these reflections will give us pause and make us ponder about the profound meaning nature has in the life of man, the more so as in this age of technology we tend to forget our ecological responsibilities. It is up to us if future generations will do more than <u>read</u> about a part of the United States of America, the Wissahickon Valley, which the author of the <u>Raven</u> described as one of "the real Edens of the land."

Philadelphia   VICTOR GROVE

A Sweet and Natural Retreat from Noise and Talk, and allows opportunity for Reflection, and gives the best Subjects for it.

William Penn, Some Fruits of Solitude

And thou, Philadelphia, the virgin settlement of this province, named before thou wert born, what love, what care, what service, and what travail have there been to bring thee forth and preserve thee from such as would abuse and defile thee. O that though mayest be kept from the evil that would overwhelm thee, that faithful to the God of thy mercies, in the life of righteousness, thou mayest be preserved to the end. My soul prays to God for thee, that thou mayest stand in the day of trial, that thy children may be blest of the Lord, and thy people saved by His power.

William Penn's Prayer, before sailing
for England in 1684

We must keep at least a few communities of
nature natural, so that we may learn more
fully, by scientific study, the lesson of
the interdependence of life and find our
place more humbly in the biosphere before
we break irreparably the chain of life
upon which our own existence hangs.

Gerard Piel, America's Living
Heritage.

Men look for God and fancy him concealed
In wonder wordings or some bush aflame.
But in earth's common things He stands revealed,
while stars and flowers and trees spell out His name.

Poet unknown.

I am convinced that civilized man needs
more than "civilization" to keep well.
The stars and planetary winds are part of
man. So are flowers, grass, trees, and
birds. Those who are raised to respect
them find with the passage of time
increasing adoration for the endless
wonders of nature. Those who are never
inducted into those mysteries and only
know the "wonders of science" have been
cheated; their spiritual growth has
been stunted.

Sigmund Freud, An Outline of
Psychoanalysis

A poem of everlasting beauty and a dream of
magnificence - the world-hidden, wood
embowered Wissahickon.

George Lippard, 1822-1854

VALLEY GREEN

The ancient values of dignity,
beauty and poetry which sustain it
are of nature's inspiration; they
are born of the mystery and beauty
of the world. Do not dishonor the
earth lest you dishonor the spirit
of man.

Henry Beston, The Outermost
House

I robbed the Woods -
The trusting Woods
The unsuspecting Trees
Brought out their Burs and Mosses
My fantasy to please.
I scanned their trinkets curious -
I grasped - I bore away -
What will the solemn Hemlock -
What will the Oak tree say?

Emily Dickinson

Rich gift of God! A year of time!
What pomp of rise and shut of day,
What hues wherewith our northern clime
Makes autumn's dropping woodlands gay,
What airs outblown from ferny dells,
And clover-bloom and sweet briar smells,
What songs of brooks and birds,
What fruits and flowers,
Green woods and moonlit snows,
Have in its round been ours.

John Greenleaf Whittier,
1807-1892
A Last Walk in Autumn

Near Wissahickon's mossy banks,
      where purling fountains glide
Beneath the Spruce's shady boughs
      and laurel's blooming pride,
Where little fishes sport and play
      diverting to the sight,
Whilst all the warbling winged race,
      afford my ear delight;
Here are evergreens by nature set,
      on which those warblers sing,
And flowery aromatic Groves
      form an eternal spring;
Refreshing breezes round me move,
      which with the blossoms play,
And balmy odors on their wings
      Through all my vale convey.

Thomas Livezey, 1765

The most beautiful and most profound emotion
we can experience is the sensation of the
mystical. It is the source of all true science.
He to whom this emotion is a stranger, who can
no longer wonder and stand rapt in awe,
is as good as dead. To know that what is
impenetrable to us really exists, manifesting
itself as the highest wisdom and the most
radiant beauty which our dull faculties can
comprehend only in their most primitive forms -
this knowledge, this feeling is at the center
of true religiousness.

Albert Einstein

24

We owe it to ourselves and to mankind
to give full rein to our instinctive love
of Natural Beauty, and to train and refine
every inclination and capacity we have for
appreciating it till wc are able to see
all those finer glories of which we now
discover only the first fine glow.

Sir Francis Younghusband,
1863-1924, Explorer

By the side of religion, by the side of science,
by the side of poetry, stands natural beauty,
not as a rival to these, but as the common
inspirer and nourisher of them all.

G.M. Trevelyan

In the wilderness life seems neither long
nor short, and we take no more heed to
save time or make haste than do the trees
and the stars. This is true freedom,
a good practical sort of immortality.

John Muir

The way a crow
Shook down on me
The dust of snow
From a hemlock tree

Has given me heart
A change of mood
And saved some part
Of a day I had rued.

Robert Frost, Dust of Snow

This curious world which we inhabit is more
wonderful than it is convenient; more
beautiful than it is useful; it is more to
be admired than to be used.

Henry D. Thoreau
From a graduation speech, while
still a student at Harvard.

If there is magic on this planet, it is
contained in water.

Loren Eiseley

On the solid ground of nature builds
the mind that rests for aye.

William Wordsworth

There are some people who can live without
wild things about them and the earth beneath
their feet, and some who cannot. To those of
us who, in a city, are always aware of the
abused and abased earth below the pavement,
walking on grass, watching the flight of birds,
or finding the first spring dandelion are
rights as old and unalienable as the rights
of life, liberty and the pursuit of happiness.
We belong to no cult, We are Nature Lovers.
We don't love nature any more than we love
breathing. Nature is simply something
indespensable, like air and light and water,
that we accept as necessary to living, and
the nearer we can get to it the happier we are.

Louise Dickenson Rich

These are things which other nations can never
recover. Should we lose them, we could not
recover them either. The generation now living
may very well be that which will make the
irrevocable decision whether or not America will
continue to be for centuries to come the one
great nation which had the foresight to preserve
an important part of its heritage. If we do not
preserve it, then we shall have diminished by
just that much the unique privilege of being
an American.

Joseph Wood Krutch.

The finest workers in stone are not
copper or steel tools, but the gentle
touches of air and water working at
leisure with a liberal allowance
of time.

Henry D. Thoreau

I deliberately shut up my books, put on my
old clothes and old hat and slink away to
the whortleberry bushes and slip with the
greatest satisfaction into a little cowpath
where I am sure I can defy observation...
I solace myself for hours with picking
blueberries and other trash of the woods,
far from fame, behind the birchtrees.
I seldom enjoy hours as I do these. I
remember them in winter; I expect them
in spring.

Ralph Waldo Emerson,
Journals, Cambridge 1828

Of our swift passage through this scenery
Of life and death, more durable than we,
What landmark so congenial as a tree
Recording the fair seasons as they flee.

James Russell Lowell

The whole land was mellow with warm sunset,
the sky soft and bright, and golden like a
dream. I stopped for a long time opposite
the Wissahickon creek. The stone bridge,
with its gray arch, mingled with the rough
blocks of rock on which it rested, the sheet
of foaming water falling like a curtain of gold
over the dam among the dark stones below, on
whose brown sides the ruddy sunlight and
glittering water fell like splinters
of light....

Fanny Kemble, 1809-1893
She discovered the Valley of the
Wissahickon on December 30, 1832
on her return from Manayunk.

Give me the splendid silent sun....
Give me solitude,
Give me Nature,
Give me again
O nature
Your primal sanities!

Walt Whitman

Sometimes the rare, the beautiful can
only emerge or survive in isolation.
In a similar manner, some degree of
withdrawal serves to nurture man's
creative powers.

Loren Eiseley

In recent decades we have slowly come back
to some of the truths that the Indians knew
from the beginning: that unborn generations
have a claim on the land equal to our own;
that man need to learn from nature, to keep
an ear to the earth, and to replenish their
spirits in frequent contacts with animals
and wild land. And most important of all,
we are recovering a sense of reverence for
the land.

Stewart L. Udall, The Quiet Crisis

To live healthily and successfully on the
land we must also live with it. We must
be part not only of the human community,
but of the whole community; we must
acknowledge some sort of oneness not only
with our neighbors, our countrymen and
our civilization but also some respect
for the natural as well as for the manmade
community... Unless we share this
terrestrial globe with creatures other
than ourselves, we shall not be able to
live on it for long.

Joseph Wood Krutch

Nature never did betray
The heart that loved her. 'tis her privilege
Through all the years of this our life, to lead
From joy to joy.

William Wordsworth, July 13, 1798

For Dr. Victor Grove, putting together *Philadelphia, A Hiker's Paradise*, meant times of joy and true relaxation--not his usual vocation of academic writing and lecturing.

Dr. Grove lectured at universities, colleges, for British and US troops, as well as for German prisoners of war. His published works include *The Language Bar*, and *Hamlet - The Drama of Modern Man*.